MODERN ENGINEERING MARVELS

WEARABLE TECHNOLOGY

Valerie Bodden

Checkerboard Library

An Imprint of Abdo Publishing
abdopublishing.com

ABDOPUBLISHING.COM

Published by Abdo Publishing, a division of ABDO, PO Box 398166, Minneapolis, Minnesota 55439.
Copyright © 2018 by Abdo Consulting Group, Inc. International copyrights reserved in all countries.
No part of this book may be reproduced in any form without written permission from the publisher.
Checkerboard Library™ is a trademark and logo of Abdo Publishing.

Printed in the United States of America, North Mankato, Minnesota
062017
092017

THIS BOOK CONTAINS
RECYCLED MATERIALS

Design: Kelly Doudna, Mighty Media, Inc.
Production: Mighty Media, Inc.
Editor: Rebecca Felix
Cover Photograph: Shutterstock
Interior Photographs: Amber Case/Flickr, p. 13; AP Images, pp. 11, 16, 17, 23, 29 (top); iStockphoto,
pp. 5, 20; Loic Le Meur/Flickr, p. 25; Maurizio Pesce/Flickr, p. 19; Mighty Media, Inc., p. 15; Rain
Rabbit/Flickr, p. 27; Shutterstock, pp. 1, 4, 7, 9, 15, 28 (top), 28 (bottom left), 28 (bottom right),
29 (bottom); Tom Faulkner/U.S. Army RDECOM/Flickr, p. 21

Publisher's Cataloging-in-Publication Data

Names: Bodden, Valerie, author.
Title: Wearable technology / by Valerie Bodden.
Description: Minneapolis, MN : Abdo Publishing, 2018. | Series: Modern
    engineering marvels.
Identifiers: LCCN 2016962797 | ISBN 9781532110924 (lib. bdg.) |
    ISBN 9781680788778 (ebook)
Subjects: LCSH: Wearable technology--Juvenile literature. Smart materials--
    Juvenile literature. |Technological innovations--Juvenile literature. |
    Inventions--Juvenile literature.
Classification: DDC 600--dc23
LC record available at http://lccn.loc.gov/2016962797

CONTENTS

1 INCREDIBLE ATTIRE

You're playing soccer with your friends. Suddenly, your shirt buzzes. Its sweat sensors have detected that you are getting **dehydrated**. You need a water break. You jog over to grab a drink. Just as you finish, your cell phone buzzes with an alert. The phone's battery is almost dead.

You're not worried. You can plug your phone into your shoes on the way home. Your footsteps will **generate** enough energy to charge the battery. This is the power of wearable **technology**!

Wearable technology is devices, **accessories**, and clothing worn on the human body. These items are electronic or computerized. They include everything from smartwatches to fitness clothing and even **robotic** suits.

TECH TIDBIT

Technology is considered "smart" when it operates automatically by electronic means, is interactive, and is connected to a network.

Wearing a smartwatch is like having a computer on your wrist! Many smartwatches can monitor your heart rate, provide navigation, and more.

Wearable devices collect and **analyze** data about users and their surroundings. Some **technologies** provide users with helpful information. Others are made to use for entertainment. With new advances, a future in which every item you wear is a cutting-edge device is closer than you think!

Some of the earliest versions of wearable **technology** were eyeglasses. The first mention of eyeglasses was recorded in Britain in 1268. But even before this, people in Europe and China wore magnifying lenses in frames to help them see better.

Next, people invented wearable timekeeping devices. The first watch was created in the 1500s and called the Nuremberg Egg. People wore the heavy, oval-shaped watch around their necks. In the late 1600s, people started using pocket watches. These watches were smaller and lighter than the Nuremberg Egg.

The first electric lightbulbs appeared in the 1880s. By 1884, the Electric Girl Lighting Company **embedded** battery-powered lightbulbs into dresses. Then, they sent young women wearing the dresses to entertain people in their homes.

Watches continued to develop too. Some people wished for one that was easier to check than the pocket watch. Pilot Alberto Santos-Dumont wanted one he could check without taking his hands off his flying machine's controls. He spoke to his friend,

Pocket watches were not well suited for action. It was difficult and distracting for the wearer to reach into his or her pocket during activities.

businessman Louis Cartier, who designed the wristwatch in 1904. During **World War I**, many soldiers wore wristwatches so they could time their attacks. By the time the war ended in 1918, wristwatches had become popular among the public as well.

ENTERTAINMENT & ADVANCES

Eyeglasses and watches were wearables meant to perform a helpful task. As **technology** advanced, inventors created the first computers in the 1940s. In 1961, math professor Edward Thorp created the first wearable computer.

Thorp's small computer fit in his shoe. He used it to cheat at a game called roulette. Roulette players bet on which number a ball on a spinning wheel will land on. Thorp tapped buttons in his shoe to indicate the wheel's speed. Then the computer sent a tone to his hearing aid telling him which number to bet on.

In the late 1960s and early 1970s, wearables entered space as the first astronauts landed on the moon. Astronaut space suits **inflated** or **deflated** to provide proper air pressure. They also had heating, cooling, and radio communication systems.

Back on Earth, designers made advancement in watches. In 1972, the Hamilton Watch Company created Pulsar, the world's first digital watch. It showed the time as lighted numbers on an electronic display.

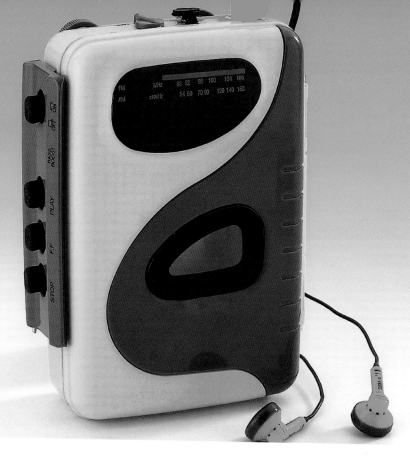

The Walkman was either carried or placed in the user's pocket. Headphones or
earbuds were attached with a wire.

By the late 1970s, developers focused on **portable** music.
In 1979, electronic and gaming corporation Sony developed the
Walkman, a portable **cassette** tape player. When CDs were
developed in the 1980s, portable CD players appeared as well.

BACKPACKS, EYE-CAMS & ACCESSORIES

Computers advanced wearable musical and timekeeping devices. In 1981, they made wearable photography devices possible. That year, Canadian high school student Steve Mann wired a computer into a backpack. Wires ran from the computer to a head-mounted display (HMD). The HMD had a camera that hung over one of Mann's eyes. Mann called his device the EyeTap.

In 1989, US company Reflection **Technology** developed the Private Eye. This wearable computer had an HMD with a small screen over the left eye. The HMD was connected to a computer central processing unit (CPU) and a large battery the user wore in a shoulder bag.

Private Eye users also wore a handheld keyboard called the Twiddler on the wrist. The Private Eye was meant to allow users to read, edit, and write documents on the go. But most users thought it was too heavy, and so the device never took off with the public.

Mann continued to improve the EyeTap in the 1990s, working to make it smaller and lighter.

The 1980s also saw the introduction of electronic clothing. In 1985, designer Harry Wainwright created a shirt that contained electronic elements. The shirt used a small computer, LED lights, and **fiber optics** to display a moving cartoon. In the 1990s, coats with this **technology** were sold at Disney theme parks.

The first messaging watch, the Seiko Receptor Message Watch, arrived in 1990. It could receive text messages using radio signals. But the watch's technology suffered from software flaws. It was discontinued in 1999.

By the late 1990s, most developers turned their attention to cell phones. The first cell phone was created in 1973. Over the years, cell phones became smaller, faster, and more powerful. Soon, designers used phone **technology** in wearable devices.

In 1998, Mann once again made news in the world of wearables. That year, he created the first wristwatch videophone. It displayed video on the watch face. A **prototype** was created, but the watch was not made widely available.

Bluetooth headsets appeared in 2000. Bluetooth allows machines to communicate wirelessly over short distances. Soon, people wore Bluetooth earpieces linked to their cell phones. This meant they could make hands-free phone calls.

Other companies focused on devices worn on the wrist. In 2003, wrist **Global Positioning System (GPS)** units hit the market. Wrist personal digital assistants (PDAs) also came out.

Wrist PDAs had touch screens that could be controlled with a **stylus**. But they had a short battery life, lasting only a day or

STEVE MANN

Steve Mann began building computer systems as a child in Canada. In 1981, Mann designed the EyeTap, a backpack computer that took photos. Mann has continued to wear an EyeTap for more than 30 years.

In 1992, Mann entered the Massachusetts Institute of Technology (MIT), where he earned a PhD in 1997. In 1998, he became a professor at the University of Toronto. That year, he created the wristwatch videophone.

Mann holds patents for many other technology and wearable inventions as well. Among his successful inventions is high dynamic range (HDR) imaging, a technology used in most cameras today. Mann is often called the father of wearable computing.

Steve Mann

so between charges. And many users felt they were too large to wear on the wrist. However, wrist **technology** would become smaller, and more popular, in the coming years.

In 2007, **entrepreneurs** James Park and Eric Friedman founded the company Fitbit. Two years later, they designed fitness trackers that clipped onto users' clothing. The devices had motion sensors that tracked the wearer's activity. In 2013, Fitbit made wristband fitness trackers. Around the same time, other companies released their own wristband fitness trackers.

In 2012, Canadian entrepreneur Eric Migicovsky released a watch called Pebble. It became the first successful smartwatch. In addition to telling the time and tracking fitness goals, Pebble interacts with apps on a user's smartphone to display alerts for e-mails, give **GPS** directions, and send text messages.

Three years later, **technology** giant Apple released its version of a smartwatch. The Apple Watch had more **capabilities** than Pebble. It could respond to voice commands, **monitor** the user's heart rate, make payments at stores, and much more. More than 12 million Apple Watches were sold in the first year.

SMARTWATCH

Today's smartwatches offer a variety of functions. Many have some or all of these basic features.

CAMERA
Cameras can snap photos from the user's wrist.

ANTENNA
A tiny Bluetooth antenna allows the smartwatch to communicate with the user's phone.

DISPLAY
Many smartwatches have color displays with touch screens. Others have black-and-white screens with push buttons on the side of the watch face.

MICROPHONE/SPEAKER
Microphones and speakers can be used to make calls. Speakers can also be used to listen to music. Microphones allow watches to respond to voice commands.

SENSORS
Sensors can track distance and speed traveled, **monitor** heart rate, and more.

BATTERY
Battery life is one of the biggest challenges for smartwatches. Most last only one to two days between charges.

Today, wristbands continue to be a popular form of fitness tracker. People use fitness trackers to learn more about themselves. These devices can calculate steps taken, heart rate, sleep quality, and more. Some even **monitor** mood and stress levels. The WellBe bracelet is one. When the bracelet detects stress, a connected app offers relaxation tips.

By the 2010s, wearable **technology** extended beyond the wrist. In 2014, Moov company created devices that were strapped on the arm or leg or **embedded** in a sweatband or swim cap. The Moov device monitors the wearer's heart rate and provides voice coaching. It also monitors form, offers tips on how to improve, and more.

New wearable fitness companies including Hexoskin, Athos, and Lumo have released

TECH TIDBIT

Sportswear company Nike released HyperAdapt shoes in 2016. The shoes' sensors interpret the wearer's foot shape and tighten to a snug fit.

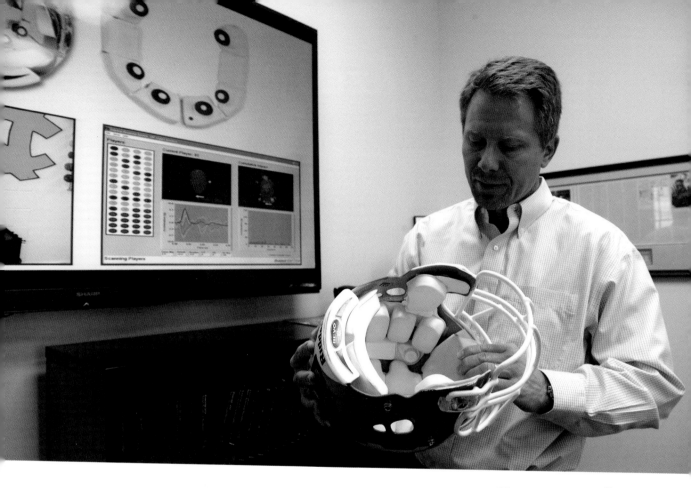

In 2015, designers created football helmets with impact sensors. The sensors monitor how hard a player gets hit, interpreting the data to help the wearer avoid head injury.

fitness tracking clothes. These tight-fitting shirts and shorts are loaded with sensors. The sensors track heart rate, muscle activity, form, and miles walked.

Computerized clothing, or smart clothes, have also been designed for uses away from the gym. In 2014, clothing designer Tommy Hilfiger launched a jacket covered with **flexible** solar panels. Energy **generated** by the solar panels was stored in a battery in the jacket's pocket. Users could plug their cell phones into the battery to charge them.

In 2016, **technology** company Samsung released a brand of computerized clothing called the Human Fit. The label included a business suit with a sensor sewn into the fabric. The sensor connects to the wearer's smartphone. It allows the wearer to open apps on their phone and more using hand gestures.

Smart clothes technology has become smaller and more powerful in recent years. But many garments are still made by simply **embedding** or attaching gadgets to cloth. In 2016, Google's Project Jacquard took smart clothes to another level.

Project Jacquard uses a special conductive yarn to create clothing that can sense touch, similar to a touch screen. Tiny

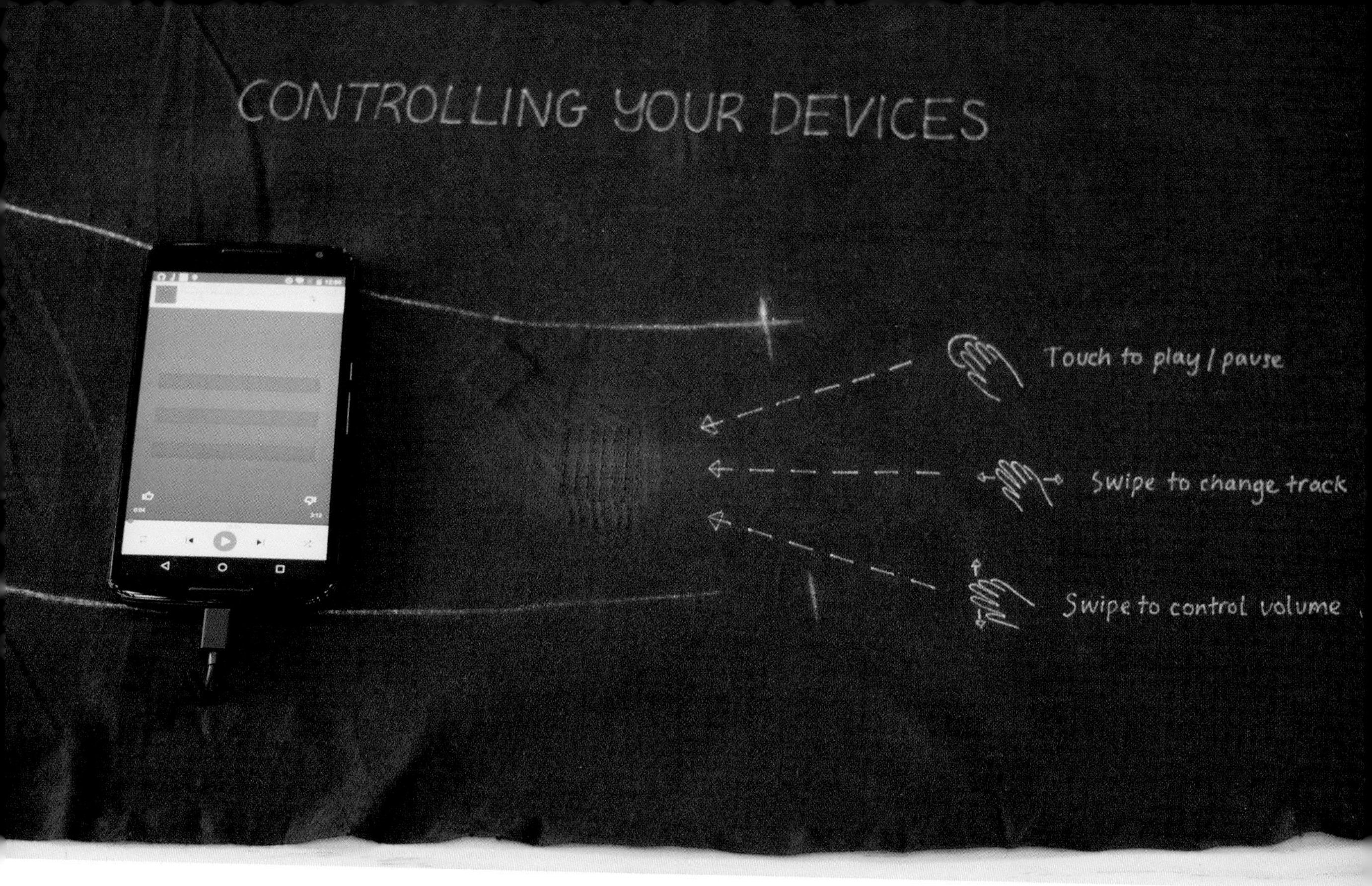

CONTROLLING YOUR DEVICES

Touch to play / pause

Swipe to change track

Swipe to control volume

The conductive yarn used by Project Jacquard can be woven to either appear on a garment or be invisible.

circuits in the clothing send signals from the cloth to the user's smartphone or another device. So swiping a shirt sleeve, for example, might control the volume of a smartphone's music. Levi's has partnered with Project Jacquard to develop denim clothing with this **technology**.

Many smart clothes contain only sections of computerized gadgetry. But some developers create full-body wearable devices. In 2014, Conor Walsh of the Wyss Institute for Biologically Inspired Engineering invented a **robotic** suit.

Walsh's soft, **flexible** suit is strapped around a user's legs. A small control box is clipped onto the user's belt or backpack. Sensors detect when the user takes a step. Then the suit uses cables and pulleys to give the user extra power for the step.

Soldiers, firefighters, and others can use this suit to help carry heavy loads. People with difficulty walking can also wear it to help them move more easily.

Medical **therapies** and treatments have also emerged in wearable **accessories**. One example is Quell. It is a band that straps

TECH TIDBIT

A smart shirt made by British company CuteCircuit hugs wearers whenever they get a text message!

to a wearer's leg to help people with chronic pain. The device **triggers** nerves that send signals to the brain. This causes the brain to block pain signals in the body.

Developers are working to create sensors that **analyze** users' sweat. These sensors could detect signs of **dehydration**. Someday, wearable devices may even provide early warning of certain diseases.

A US soldier is fitted with Walsh's soft robotic suit for testing.

WEARABLE IDENTITY & TRACKING

Developers have created several wearables to monitor the way the wearer feels. Others are working to create devices that manage who the wearer is. These devices can be used to track a person's identity.

At Disney World in Orlando, Florida, guests wear a wristband. The wristband works as their ticket to rides. It is also the key to their hotel room and can even be used to pay for food.

A company called Ringly designed a smart ring. It lights up or vibrates when the wearer receives a call or an e-mail. The NFC Ring is a smart ring that can unlock specially made door locks.

Wearables can also help keep children safe in a crowd. KiLife Tech has created the MyKid Pod and Kiband bracelets. These bracelets can be strapped to children's arms. Each bracelet has a Bluetooth link to the parent's phone. If the child wanders too far from the parent, the bracelet makes a loud sound as a warning.

Wearable gadgets can also be used to track a pet's identity and activity. Many companies have created **GPS** devices that

WonderWoof is a device attached to a pet's collar. It tracks the pet's daily activities and location.

attach to a pet's collar. Nuzzle is one such device. It connects to a pet owner's cell phone and sends continually updated data on his or her pet's location. This way, if a pet dog or cat runs away, its owner can find it right away!

From medical **therapies** to pet tracking, fitness watches to touch screen cloth, modern wearables are amazing. Someday, people may dress in devices every day. Designers are continually working to create more advanced gadgets and garments.

California company Meta is working to develop a commercial version of Mann's EyeTap. In 2012, Google created Google Glass. These glasses could display websites and maps and make phone calls. In 2015, Google discontinued Glass for a product redesign.

In 2016, social media company Snapchat released Spectacles. The glasses have a small camera that records video of what the wearer sees. The video is uploaded to their Snapchat followers.

New designs are also in the works for smart clothes. Some developers are working to create clothes that carry their own wireless Internet hot spot or electric charging stations. A special stretchable ink might serve as wires in these clothes.

Other future smart clothes might make use of tiny **drones**. A drone would rest on a person's clothing when not in use. For

Google Glass responds to voice commands beginning with "Okay, Glass." For example, wearers can snap a photo simply by saying, "Okay, Glass, take a photo."

example, a **drone** might **monitor** pollution levels while sitting on a person's shoulder. If pollution reached unsafe levels, the drone would hover in front of the person's face to filter the air.

Someday, just moving may be enough to power wearable devices. Massachusetts Institute of **Technology** (MIT) scientists are working to create shoes that serve as power stations. When users walk or run, these shoes would convert the energy **generated** by the movement into electricity. Users could charge their devices by plugging them into the shoes.

Wearable devices are likely to get smaller, too. Someday, instead of wearables, people may use "invisibles." These see-through sensors would be attached to the skin like an invisible tattoo. They could then be used to **monitor** the user's health, make payments, unlock doors, and more.

Visible temporary tattoos that work this way are already in the works. MIT engineers have developed a process called DuoSkin. This process is used to create custom devices that are attached directly to the skin like a temporary tattoo. DuoSkin can be programmed to connect to smartphones, computers, and other devices.

Some designers dream of making the entire surface of the human body into a computer. They are working on creating an e-skin. This skin would allow users to see a computer display on their arms. Their arms could even work as a touch screen!

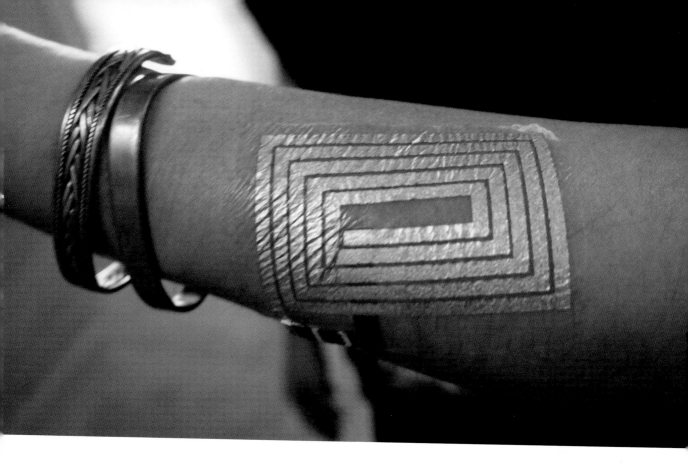

DuoSkin tattoos are made from gold metal leaf. This material is conductive and can interact with an electronic circuit.

What **technologies** will you wear in the future? You may wear your computer on your head, or answer your smartphone by blinking. As technology advances, anything is possible!

TECH TIMELINE

1500s
The Nuremberg Egg, a heavy timepiece worn around the neck, is created.

1904
Louis Cartier designs the wristwatch.

1972
The Hamilton Watch Company releases the first digital watch.

1268
The first mention of eyeglasses is recorded in Britain.

1961
Edward Thorp creates the first wearable computer and uses it to cheat at roulette.

1981

Steve Mann creates the EyeTap.

2007

James Park and Eric Friedman found Fitbit. They release their first fitness trackers two years later.

1990

The Seiko Receptor Message Watch uses radio signals to receive messages.

2000

Bluetooth headsets make wireless, hands-free phone calls possible.

2015

Apple Watch sells 12 million units in its first year.

GLOSSARY

accessory–a small item worn with clothing, such as a belt or ring.

analyze–to determine the meaning of something by breaking down its parts.

capability–the power or ability to do something.

cassette–a plastic cartridge containing magnetic tape with the tape passing from one reel to another to play audio or video.

deflate–to let the air or gas out of something.

dehydrated–the state a person is in when he or she has lost a large amount of water from the body.

drone–an aircraft without a pilot that is controlled remotely.

embed–to put something inside something else in a way that it cannot be easily removed.

entrepreneur–one who organizes, manages, and accepts the risks of a business or an enterprise.

fiber optics–flexible, thin fibers that transmit light signals.

flexible–able to bend or move easily.

generate–to create or produce something.

Global Positioning System (GPS)–a space-based navigation system used to pinpoint locations on Earth.

inflate–to expand by filling with air or a gas.

monitor–to watch, keep track of, or oversee.

portable–able to be carried easily.

prototype–an early model of a product on which future versions can be modeled.

robotic–having features or elements of a robot.

stylus–a small stick used to input data on devices.

technology–a capability given by the practical application of knowledge.

therapy–relating to the treatment of diseases and disorders.

trigger–to cause something to happen immediately.

World War I–from 1914 to 1918, fought in Europe. Great Britain, France, Russia, the United States, and their allies were on one side. Germany, Austria-Hungary, and their allies were on the other side.

WEBSITES

To learn more about Modern Engineering Marvels, visit **abdobooklinks.com**. These links are routinely monitored and updated to provide the most current information available.

INDEX